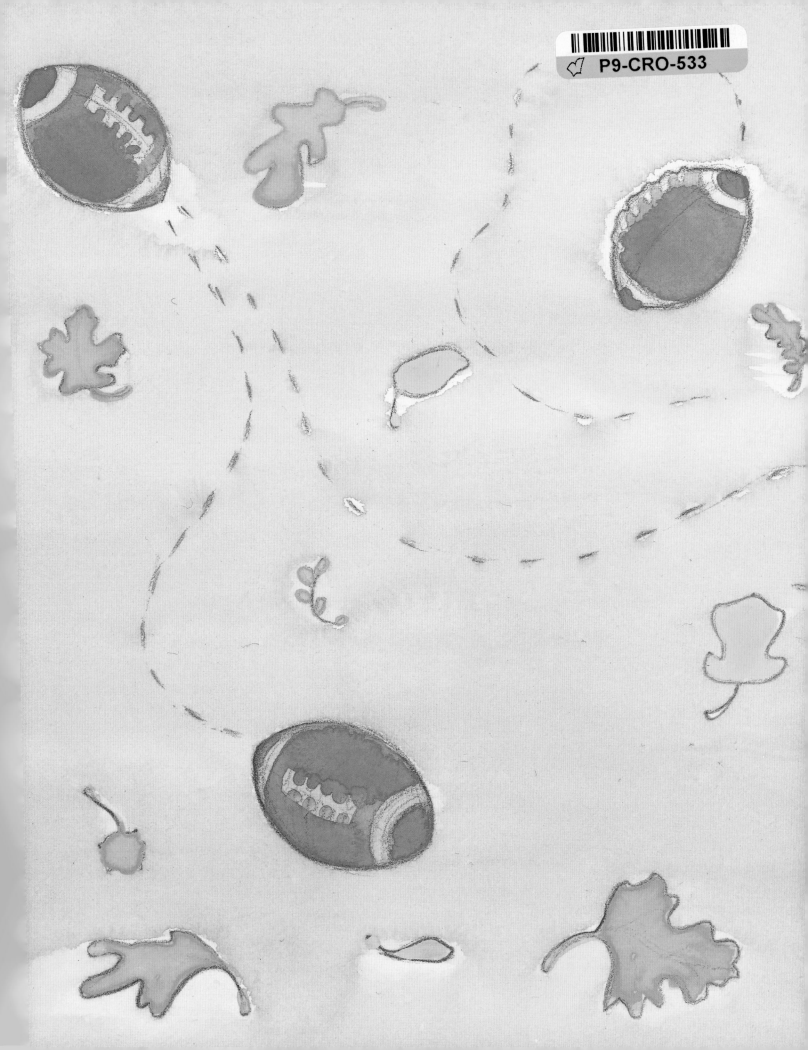

Commit to the Lord whatever you do,
and your plans will succeed.

PROVERBS 16:3 (NIV)

To my parents, Wilbur and CleoMae Dungy, who helped us to dream.
And to my wife, Lauren, who is doing the same for our children —T. D.

To Will, John, Tay, and the Toad—my "little" brothers —A. J. B.

LITTLE SIMON INSPIRATIONS
An imprint of Simon & Schuster Children's Publishing Division
1230 Avenue of the Americas, New York, New York 10020
Text copyright © 2008 by Tony Dungy. Illustrations copyright © 2008 by Amy June Bates.
Published in association with the literary agency of Legacy, LLC, Winter Park, FL 32789.
All rights reserved, including the right of reproduction in whole or in part in any form.
LITTLE SIMON INSPIRATIONS is a registered trademark of Simon & Schuster, Inc., and associated
colophon is a trademark of Simon & Schuster, Inc. Manufactured in China
0317 SCP
8 10 9 7
Library of Congress Cataloging-in-Publication Data
Dungy, Tony. You can do it / by Tony Dungy ; illustrated by Amy June Bates. — 1st ed. p. cm.
Summary: Faith and the support of a loving family help Linden when he is upset over being
the only one in his class or at home who does not know what he wants to be when he grows up.
ISBN-13: 978-1-4169-5461-3   ISBN-10: 1-4169-5461-9 [1. Ability—Fiction. 2. Family life—Fiction. 3. Schools—Fiction.
4. Christian life—Fiction.] I. Bates, Amy June, ill. II. Title. PZ7.D9187You 2008   [E]—dc22   2007042313

You Can Do It!

By Tony Dungy

Illustrated by Amy June Bates

LITTLE SIMON INSPIRATIONS

New York   London   Toronto   Sydney   New Delhi

Tony's little brother, Linden, was having a bad day at school.

To begin with, his tooth hurt. A lot.

And then in the middle of class Linden touched his sore cheek, and he accidentally made a big, loud noise that sounded like . . . a duck quacking. Everyone started laughing at him. Except his teacher, Mrs. Lee, who said his parents could expect a call tonight.

All this made it hard for Linden to concentrate on the lesson. Mrs. Lee went around the room asking everyone what they dreamed of being someday.

When it was Linden's turn, he realized he was the only one who had no idea.

"I don't know," he answered. "Maybe a duck?"

Everyone started laughing again. Linden liked it when he made people smile, but Mrs. Lee was not smiling.

He couldn't wait until the bell rang so he could walk home with his big brother, Tony.

Tony tried to cheer up Linden on the way home.

"Hey, Linden, why don't you go out for a long pass just like I taught you?" Tony called out as he pulled the football from under his arm.

The ball spiraled through the air in a perfect arch and landed in Linden's arms with a soft thud. Linden waved the ball proudly.

"Maybe someday I'll be as good in sports as you are," he said to Tony as they continued to walk home. Linden knew his brother hoped to become a football player when he grew up. Tony could already throw a football so far and high, you might as well pack a snack to eat while waiting for it to come back down.

Tony playfully punched Linden's arm. "That's cool, little brother, but remember what Mom and Dad always tell us. . . ."

"I know, I know," Linden said. "Whatever it is that you want to do, you can do it. Trust God and dream big!" But Linden wondered if playing football was really what he wanted to do.

"That was Mrs. Lee again," Linden's dad said as he hung up the phone.

"What did he do this time?" Linden's mom asked. "Was he quacking like a duck during math again?"

"Actually, no," Dad replied. "This time it was in English class."

"Oh, no," Mom sighed, then added, "but you have to admit he does a great duck call!"

"That he does," agreed Dad as they watched the boys race to the house behind their sisters, Sherri and Lauren. "But he should not be doing it in the middle of class."

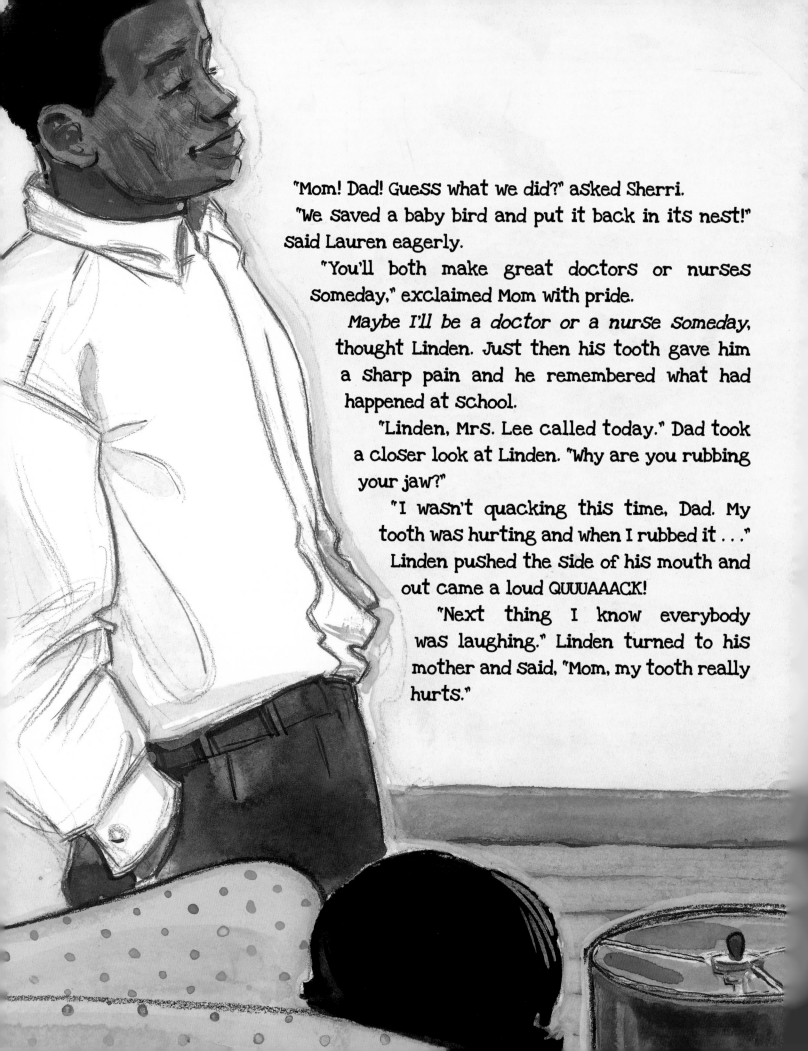

"Mom! Dad! Guess what we did?" asked Sherri.

"We saved a baby bird and put it back in its nest!" said Lauren eagerly.

"You'll both make great doctors or nurses someday," exclaimed Mom with pride.

Maybe I'll be a *doctor or a nurse someday*, thought Linden. Just then his tooth gave him a sharp pain and he remembered what had happened at school.

"Linden, Mrs. Lee called today." Dad took a closer look at Linden. "Why are you rubbing your jaw?"

"I wasn't quacking this time, Dad. My tooth was hurting and when I rubbed it . . ." Linden pushed the side of his mouth and out came a loud QUUUAAACK!

"Next thing I know everybody was laughing." Linden turned to his mother and said, "Mom, my tooth really hurts."

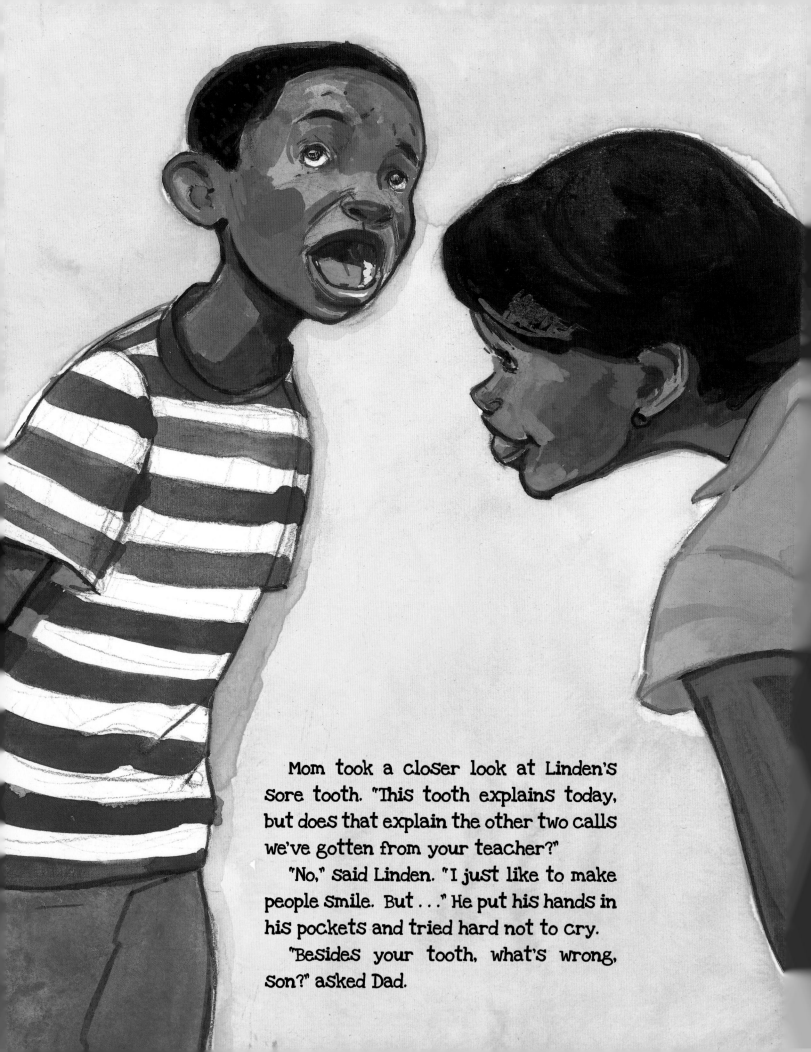

Mom took a closer look at Linden's sore tooth. "This tooth explains today, but does that explain the other two calls we've gotten from your teacher?"

"No," said Linden. "I just like to make people smile. But . . ." He put his hands in his pockets and tried hard not to cry.

"Besides your tooth, what's wrong, son?" asked Dad.

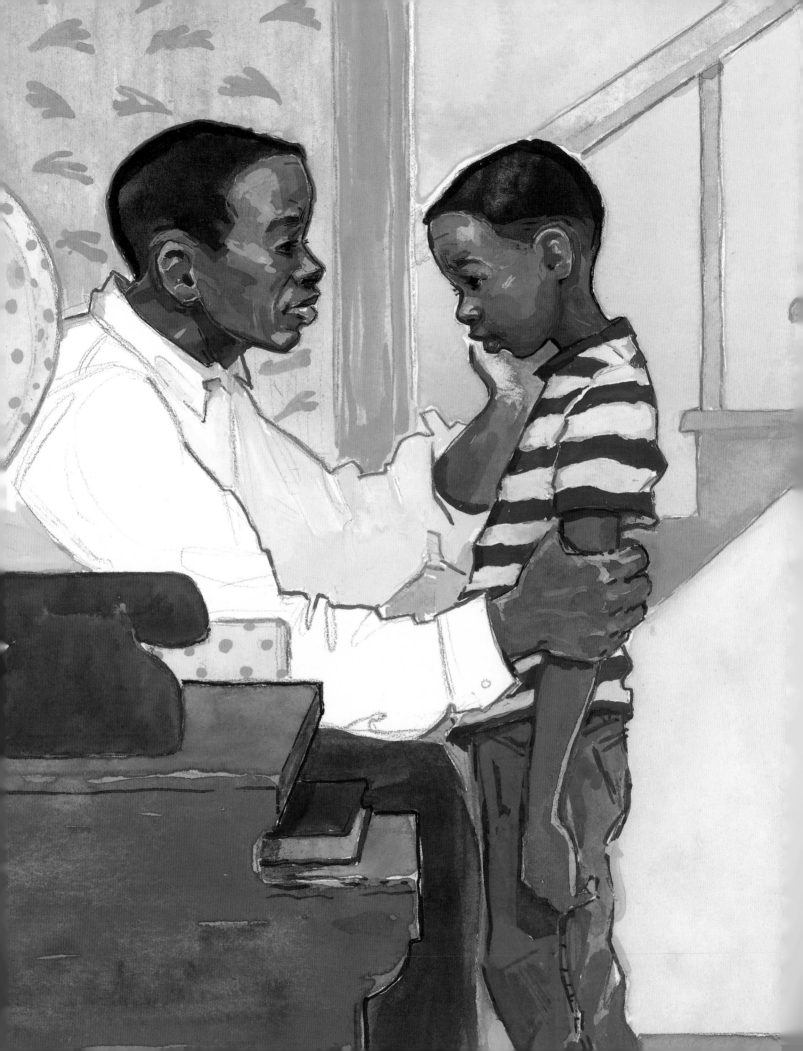

"It's just that Tony and Sherri and Lauren know their *it*. And I don't know my *it*."

"Their *it*?" asked his dad.

"Their *it*, what they dream about, what they want to be. It's like you always tell me, 'You can do it. Dream big.' But I don't know what *it* is.

"Don't you worry about that, son. I promise you, you'll find your dream in your own time. For now let's put something on that tooth to make you feel better, and we'll get you fixed up in the morning."

But Dad could see that Linden was still feeling down.

How can I make this better? he thought. *How can I help Linden find his dream?*

It was Tony's turn to say the dinner prayer and that night's was extra special.

"Dear Lord, thank You for blessing us the way You do. Thank You for the food and thank You for our dreams. And God," Tony said with his head bowed and his eyes closed extra tight, "please help Linden find his *it*. Amen!"

"What are you thinking about?" Tony asked, tossing a pillow across the room before bedtime. "Is your tooth still hurting you?"

"A little," answered Linden, "but I was thinking about your prayer tonight, Tony. I trust God. I pray every day, too, but I still don't know . . . what is my big dream?"

"I'm not sure, Linden, but God knows. And one day you will too," said Tony. "But I do know one thing you will be when you grow up."

"Really? You do?" Linden said anxiously.

"Yeah, no matter what you do or how big you get, you'll still be my baby brother!" Tony teased. "And as my baby brother you have to go to bed before me! Good night, Linden!"

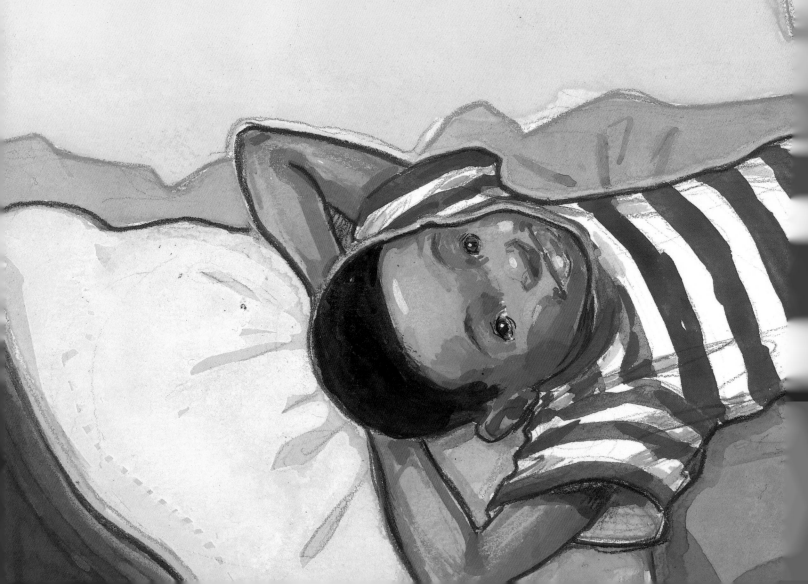

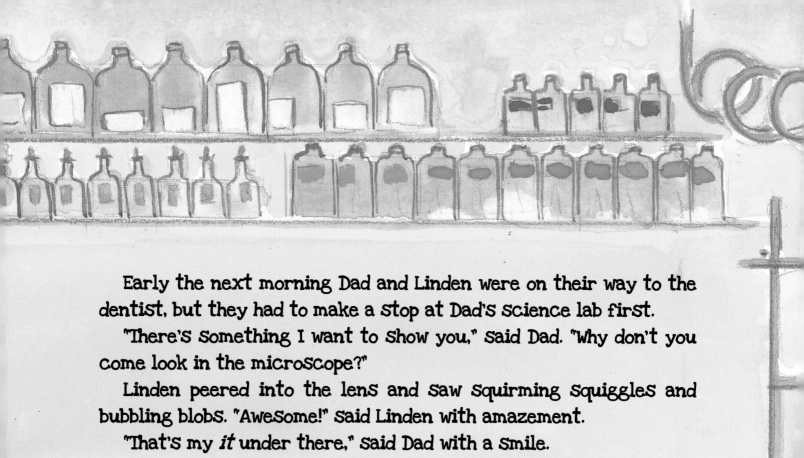

Early the next morning Dad and Linden were on their way to the dentist, but they had to make a stop at Dad's science lab first.

"There's something I want to show you," said Dad. "Why don't you come look in the microscope?"

Linden peered into the lens and saw squirming squiggles and bubbling blobs. "Awesome!" said Linden with amazement.

"That's my *it* under there," said Dad with a smile.

"Huh?" asked Linden.

"Your *it* is what you love to do. And it's something God has given you the talent to do. That's what makes it so special. Son, sometimes dreams are as big as the ocean or as small as a microbe. With faith and hard work you'll recognize your *it* someday. I didn't realize science was my *it* when I was your age . . ."

"Really? So I still have time to figure it out?" asked Linden, feeling relieved.

"Plenty of time," answered Dad. "Just keep having faith."

"One cavity filled and good as new," said Dr. Clarke.

"That's it?" said Linden with amazement and relief. "That didn't hurt at all!"

He ran his tongue over the smooth surface now filling the top of the tooth that had been causing him so much pain. He gave Dr. Clarke a big smile.

"That's what I like to see!" said Dr. Clarke. "I love to make people smile."

"Me too!" said Linden.

"You're good to go, Linden, unless you have some questions for me."

Linden had lots of questions!

"How did you squish that stuff into my tooth? And what's that tube thing? And what's that machine?"

"One question at a time," laughed Dr. Clarke, picking up a giant set of plastic teeth. "How about we start with these?"

A few weeks later it was show-and-tell day at school. Linden stood in front of the class and explained some of the amazing things he'd learned from Dr. Clarke.

"When you make people feel good, they smile. And that's why when I grow up," Linden said, "I want to be a dentist."

He winked at Tony who was watching from the doorway.

"Good for you, Linden!" said Mrs. Lee. "I think you can do it."

"I know you can do it, little brother," said his very proud, big brother Tony.

And he did.

I'M GLAD I HAD PARENTS THAT HELPED US TO DREAM. I'm glad they taught us to pray about things that were on our mind. And I'm really glad that God answers our prayers. Sometimes He answers them in unexpected ways and at unexpected times, but He's always listening to us.

Our parents taught us to dream, but they also taught us something more important. Whatever we dreamed about, we should tell God because He is the one that can make those plans succeed.

Oh, and you're probably wondering, did my brother really become a dentist? He really did! We knew he would have faith to find his dream.

And you can do it, too!